Harmoniously Hopeful

Zowie Norris

Copyright © 2024 Zowie Norris

All rights reserved.

ISBN: **9798324575304**

DEDICATION

I dedicate this book to all my family
and friends who have brought harmony
to my life - and have always given me hope.
Love you all.

Life is a song that is sung with harmony and hope.

(Not everyone is singing the same note and has the same reason for singing either!)

CONTENTS

Introduction   8

1 <u>**Kind and Optimistic**</u>

- To My Future Self — 13
- Sifting the Sands of Time — 14
- Kind, Beautiful Soul — 15
- A plea for the Dream-Maker — 16
- Hate Victim — 19
- Friendship Hope — 20
- Unforgettable Forgiveness — 21
- You only sing when you're winning! — 22

2 <u>**Self-belief and Self-love**</u>

- Just Be You! — 24
- An Apology Letter — 26
- Brain Break — 27
- Word Nerd — 28
- I'm sick of feeling sick! — 29
- The Tale of the Fading Social Butterfly — 31
- Just Stop! — 32
- What's Going Down? — 33

3   **Managing Emotions**

- The Ballad of the Storm Maker — 36
- Medellin Menopause — 37
- The Rhythm of the Rain — 39
- Destined for Heaven — 40
- Flowers no longer grow here. — 41
- The Sea's Rebellion — 42
- I'd rather … — 43
- Hater's Gonna Hate — 45
- What on earth!? — 46
- Civilised Chaos! — 47

5   **Resilience & Risk-taking**

- The paradox of change and peace — 50
- So Long Summer — 51
- Flying High — 52
- The rise and fall of the Woman warrior — 53
- Thrills and Chills — 55
- Gradually Healing — 56

6   **Happiness and Harmony**

- Harmoniously Hopeful — 58
- Bucket List Epiphany — 59
- Autumn Daze — 61
- Derbyshire Hiking Hysteria — 62
- November Nights — 64
- Rocking Out — 65
- Hibernating Heart — 66
- Gigglebox — 69
- Italian Adventures — 70

7 **Hope & Gratitude**

- Grateful Gardens — 72
- Darling Daughters — 74
- Sisterly Love — 75
- Thank You For The Music — 76
- To My Unpoetic Hubby — 77
- Celebrate the things so great. — 78
- Dad — 79
- Hope Springs Eternal — 80

8 **About the Author** — 81

My Introduction - 'Poetry Style'

Ballad of the Harmoniously Hopeful

Brimming with excitement, I'm here today
To share with you, in my humble way,
The title of my newborn creation,
A poetry anthology, ripe for celebration.

A sequel to my first venture,
Continuing the themes that quench your thirst,
Hope, positivity, realism intertwined,
Crafted to heal the soul and mind.

With each new work, I strive to ascend,
To refine my craft, to transcend.
Even if poetry isn't your chosen genre,
I'd love for you to ponder and wander.

An offering for every heart awaits,
From rhymes to soulful contemplative states,
With every word, optimism subtly flows,
A symphony of emotion that flows and grows.

The artwork on the cover, concealed for now,
Will soon be unveiled with a grand bow.
For now, I present to you, with a hopeful note,
'Harmoniously Hopeful' - a new book I wrote.

Z Norris

I am so proud and excited to be sharing my next poetry anthology with you all! My 'poetic journey' has changed so much throughout my life - but I just can't stop writing at the moment! Poetry has been in and out of my life realistically since my college days - but more frequently since the pandemic. It's crazy to think that it took a pandemic for me to make some career changes and start writing again!

Initially, I wrote poetry to inform and describe something. Possibly, because I spend most of my days doing this as a Primary School teacher!

However, although I enjoy many parts of my life - it can be devastating and challenging at times, so -writing poetry has also become a great way to express my feelings, regulate my emotions and try to make sense of different situations that I have been faced with.

Although writing poems in this way has always been personal to me - this all changed when I bravely decided to share a poem on my author page one day - quite a personal one too, about losing my mum. I was overwhelmed by the response that I received - so many people related to the poem and found comfort in my words - so I shared another one the following week and have continued to do so, over the last two years!

Unfortunately, during some of the most devastating and challenging times in your life - the people closest to you show their true colours. Don't get me wrong - some of my friends and closest family have been an amazing support, but regardless of this - my emotions and self-confidence were extremely low. It was at this time, when I began to practise some positive mindset techniques - and I believe that they also helped me to stay strong and refocus on what I loved doing - creating! Starting the day with a positive affirmation and focusing on good things - however small they may be. Finding humour no matter what the situation and turning any failures into lessons - I've definitely learned what 'not' to do or be like from many of these lessons! Attempting to transform negative self-talk into a more positive way of thinking was also part of this focus. This doesn't mean that you think everything is lovely and happy all the time - it's about finding acceptance, inner peace and ways to 'dance in the rain'. The final part of this practice is about gratitude and finding something to be thankful for everyday - and again, this can be an everyday thing from a beautiful flower that grows in your garden - to enjoying a good cup of tea.

As I began writing poetry again during this time, the themes also became about encouraging and practising having a positive mindset- which resulted in the birth of my first poetry anthology- 'Positively Poetic'.

In this anthology, I continue to build on the themes' including a focus on having hope and gaining harmony in our lives. Poems are organised under the following headings:

1) Kind and Optimistic
2) Self-belief & Self-love
3) Managing Emotions
4) Resilience & Risk-taking
5) Happiness & Harmony
6) Hope & Gratitude

On the whole, hope is viewed as a positive emotion associated with the motivation to change existing conditions. It's an important thread that runs throughout my poetry - providing my motivation to write, express my feelings and emotions and make sense of things - from small everyday situations to many global issues.

In psychology, harmony refers to a positive state of inner peace, calmness, and balance, as well as the feeling of being tuned with the world. In the social sciences, it is used to describe a pattern of relationships within a social group and between individuals and their social context. Having positive mindsets for peace, involves cultivating attitudes of empathy, compassion, and open-mindedness- all themes that I have explored through my poetry. By embracing diversity and recognising humanity in others, I believe that we can overcome prejudice, build bridges, and foster a better understanding and stronger sense of tolerance.

Life cannot be harmonious all the time, but with a positive mindset, we can learn to manage it emotionally, stay well mentally, and always remain hopeful - no matter what.

My hope for the readers of my poetry is that you are able to find enjoyment, be able to relate to the themes covered and are able to reflect and approach different situations in life, with a more positive mindset too.

Kind and Optimistic

"Keep your face towards the sunshine and the shadows will fall behind you"

Walt Whitman

To My Future Self

There will be a day when shapes do shift,
When I'll be you, and I will drift.
What will kindle the flame, I ponder,
What will be the essence, I wonder?

Will your vigor still be as a fiery tower,
Or will you have time to appreciate the flower?
May you look back with a gentle smile,
Recalling memories that stretch a mile.

I hope you still wear your vibrant attire,
Ignite the world with your internal fire.
Spend precious moments with your kin,
But also find peace within.

For your daughters, you'll always be their guide,
Yet they'll need their own space, their own stride.
May you still harbor dreams in your nook,
Still pen lines, still lose yourself in a book.

I hope you dance and sing your heart's song,
Bake delights and enjoy music all day long.
May you beam with pride, standing tall,
Reflect on the victories, big and small.

Let your time with loved ones be ever rich
Strolling down memory lane without a glitch
May your kindness and patience never sway,
Even through life's storms, come what may.

Through change and tide, please stay tender,
In life's symphony, remain a kind contender.

Sifting the Sands of Time

Time passes by before you know it !
So don't try to tell me that
I have to spend it all working
Because there are many reasons -
To experience and accomplish everything
And I'm not planning for every hour and minute
The time I have will be enjoyed
Instead it will be used well -
To appreciate and celebrate life
My life isn't a schedule - I need
To devote most of my time to others,
Instead, I will not waste the time -it's
A blessing- to feel grateful for.
I don't believe that achieving happiness is not
A Grand gesture - to complete a bucket-list, as
Life slips by quickly, so ensure you make
A million memories to cherish
Sifting through the sands of time -

(Now read from the bottom upwards
for a different viewpoint)

Kind, Beautiful Soul

Kindness has no colour, it's pure as the snow
Kindness has no gender, yet it's stronger than we know
It loves who it loves, it's gentle and it's tender
In its presence, even the toughest hearts surrender.

Kind beautiful soul, you're a sight to behold
Your beauty is within, it's deeper than gold,

Kindness does not judge, it doesn't hesitate
Kindness does not discriminate, it just loves to relate
It accepts who you are, it's patient and does not irritate
Even in the darkest times, it's a light that resonates.

Kind beautiful soul, you're a beacon in the cold
Your love is a story that's forever told

Kindness always listens, it tries to understand
If you are in trouble, it always stops to lend a hand
It isn't perfect, but it's loyal and dutiful
Not always outwardly pretty , but a kind soul is beautiful

Kind beautiful soul, you're a testament of love uncontrolled
You're not just a sight. If you're a colour - you'd be gold!

Here's to the kind beautiful souls, loyal and dutiful
May we all strive to be kind and truly beautiful.

A plea for the Dream maker

Once, I was a child, small and innocent,
Free, bold and wild was my temperament,
I danced to the rhythm of a carefree life,
A joyous bubble, absent of strife.

Imagination was my tool,
Bravery and creation made me rule,
To non-existing places, I would drift,
Laugh, love, dance to ignite a mood lift.

Dream maker, come sprinkle your magic,
Dream maker, prevent oncoming tragic
Dream maker, please grant me my dreams,
Please let them flow like sparkly streams.

Youth's flight was swift and sly,
Fun times, like birds, flew high.
Work, no play, became the norm,
Settling for jobs, just to conform.

But, oh!
This wasn't the dream's form!
It doesn't make your heart beam,
This wasn't the dream of your dream!

Dream maker, come sprinkle your magic,
Dream maker, prevent oncoming tragic
Dream maker, please grant me my dreams,
Please let them flow like sparkly streams.

Hate Victim

Don't be a victim of this foolish bully game
Joining in with nastiness -makes you just as lame!
Wicked words that whip sores of shame
To forge false friendships and fake fame.

Your words are weapons in this crime,
That pierce my heart, time after time
Yet sadly, you think your actions are fine,
Entertaining yourself at the expense of mine!

I'm trying my best to understand why, I
You feel it's your duty to make me cry,
When your own true feelings are just a lie
Who's stolen a piece of your humble pie?

Yet still you continue to go out of your way
To taunt and tease me day after day
Like I'm some monster you've hunted to slay
Poisoned and pouncing, like a predator's prey!

Your friends are there as they fear they're next
Feeding and stroking your ego that's flexed
Laughing at all the lies you talk and text
Always out for a fight , viscous and vexed

I'm sorry that you feel so much hate
But you've got no right to discriminate
A decision that's not yours to debate
Looking for enemies instead of a mate

Let's all stand up and be strong
Its gone on now for far too long
No more lashings from your tongue
You need to realise-bullying is wrong!

Friendship Hope

When life is sometimes low,
A friend can give you hope
To pull you right out
Of that slippery slope.

If you're feeling lost
Don't know where to go..
A friendly face is a place
You'll recognise and know.

When honesty is needed
In times of doubt
A friend will be kind but
The truth will come out.

A true friend can be precious,
The feeling is mutual too
Make you smile and feel great
Will always want the best for you.

Unforgettable Forgiveness

Smile sweetly at my face
Whilst I remove the knife
You stabbed in my back.

Spread your carefully selected lies
To your guidable woolly flock
Igniting a smoky, slanderous attack!

Unfortunately , I also fell
Under your hypnotic charm,
Fake smiles and flawless enthusiasm.

But you couldn't naturally retain it.
Sarcasm and challenge followed
Requests for your help, resulted in spasm.

You always played a victim
Of the poison that you poured
Dramatic enough to be awarded BAFTA .

But - I'll naïvely forgive you
My new book has started now
Our story ends 'Happily never after.'

You only sing when you're winning!

In this vast world we inhabit,
A planet so grand,
Where each soul vies for triumph,
Each life has a plan.

Amidst the daily hustle,
the struggle, the strife,
I refuse to sing that song.
I choose a different life.

I wish for you victories too,
More than the stars in the night,
I yearn for happiness for all
A soul's purest light.

May your achievements be many,
Your sorrows be few,
In your moments of glory,
My joy will ensue.

When you're winning, I'll sing
I'll cheer and applaud loudly.
Peace and harmony is my anthem,
I'll admire your success proudly.

But what, may you ask,
Does this friendship bestow?
What does this cheerleader
In your life's show know?

Ah, the return is but simple,
A joy so immense,
To watch your victory
The pleasure is intense.

The joy of your accomplishment,
The sheer thrill of your gain,
Echoes in my contented heart,
Playing a melodious refrain.

SELF-BELIEF & SELF LOVE

"Never bend your head. Hold it high. Look the world straight in the eye."

Helen Keller

Just Be You!

In the realm of whispers and false accusations,
Where ulterior motives are a common conversation,
I strive for kindness, pure and clear,
Yet some choose not to hold it dear.

Not all hearts cheer in joyous praise,
Some smiles are facades, a subtle haze.
If success is won, false friends appear,
With enemies lurking, cloaked in fear.

They weave a web of sabotage and deceit,
To mar any good, in covert conceit.
Honesty and truth, a beacon in the dark,
Call forth scammers and liars, eager to embark.

They pledge support, once the fires are lit,
A dance of shadows, in falsehood they sit.
Jealousy and bitterness, critics strive to coax,
But not their words, your life's goal hoax.

Hold fast to kindness, honesty in your heart,
Success is your journey, your own unique art.
Smile and be true, for the world to see,
If you're happy, let it be your decree.

Envious souls may strive to interrupt your serenity,
But let not their whispers change your smile's identity.
The good you do today, may be forgotten tomorrow,
So just be you, in joy and sorrow.

Embrace your style, let it unfurl,
In the grand dance of life, let it twirl.
For the world may forget, in the blink of an eye,
But you'll remember, under the endless sky.

An apology letter

Dear me,
In your mirror of remorse,
I pen a message, a route to re-course.
In incessant worry, in undue stress,
I've let others dictate my progress.
And in the silent night, my sleep I've defied,
With fretful toil, till ill-health I've espied.
I'm sorry for the doubt, the disbelief,
The self-deprecating, ever-lasting grief.
I didn't trust in your instinctive might,
But chose to cloud you in self-doubt's night.
In your professional prowess, you felt an imposter,
Despite the years of training, the wisdom you foster.
I regret the neglect, the lack of care,
Realising your worth, only after wear and tear.
A promise I make, to love you more,
To prioritise you, to let your spirit soar.
With love, from the heart that beats in your chest,

Here's to you,
dear me

PS: (time for some rest!)

Brain Break

Pounding drums control my head,
Pulsing veins vibrate my ears,
My brain's on information overload
I'm smiling through tired tears.

Sheer exhaustion is a killer,
It tests response and blows your mind
So ready for a week's brain break,
To relax, recover , rest- unwind.

Time to switch off from teaching
Any daily stresses and strife
Spend quality time with loved ones
Be a friend, a sister, mum and wife.

'Mrs Norris' is now off duty
This term's been far from steady
Proud of my class's progress
For half term - we're all so ready!

Word Nerd

Are you a lover of language and linguistics?
A finder of vocabulary you've never heard?
Been accused of swallowing a dictionary?
A loose-lipped logophile - a word nerd?

Then let me express my admiration
Whether a word-wizard or a google-geek
For your tantalising, tongue-twisting talent
Why settle for common when there's unique!

I love to listen to your rhymes and rhythm
Swaying syllables, perfectly and phonetically
Crashing in onomatopoeia- ouch!
Unscramble and line up alphabetically!

Metaphorically putting your foot in your mouth
Easily done, without accurate communication
Languages, information, formal and slang
Love's invisible words, known by the nation

Written notes, lists, poems and books,
Vastness of vocabulary- a collective herd
Emotive, expressive, ancient and new
It's wisely wonderful to be a word nerd!

I'm sick of feeling sick!

A pesky germ has taken over my body
Controlling me for a couple of days
Can anyone find the antibody?
My head's in a horrendous haze!

Strength and sanity have been kidnapped!
Extra facial fluid flows -as I weep
Any energy I had -has been zapped
All my body wants to do is sleep!

In the few hours that it I'm conscious,
More aches, pains begin to kick in,
There must be a traffic jam in my bronchus,
As I'm struggling to breathe oxygen in!

What a hullabaloo! I have no time for you!
I need to get better real quick!
Please leave my body - go on now- shoo!
I'm so sick of feeling sick!

The Tale of the Fading Social Butterfly

Once upon a time, the wistful whims were filled with joy,
In youthful days of innocence, when life was but a toy.
Playfully passionate, lusty tones, an open heart yet barred,
In meaningless connections, the self in others is scarred.

The butterfly, social in flight, its wings once vibrant and bright,
Now wounded, lonely, existing in the dimming twilight.
Its spirit, weathered by the storm, tired to its very core,
Decades wasted resisting love, a truth hard to ignore.

Wrapped in fear, the truth was clear, in exchanges so superficial,
Empty memories echoed in a silence so artificial.
Heart unbroken, yet no one near, a solitude so stark,
The butterfly, once social, now fades into the dark.

Risky past behaviour, emotions tethered in despair,
Calculated endeavours, a hollow life now bare.
The butterfly, once radiant, its wings now faded and thin,
A tale that whispers gently, of a life that could have been.

Just Stop!

Some days feel heavy on your soul,
Any plan seems like a daunting curse.
There's no shame in change -make it your goal,
Going ahead will result in feeling worse.

Remember that it's ok to not want to play
A rest is not the herald of defeat.
Don't brand it a failure - it's just a day!
Merely a quiet and kind retreat.

If the mountain looms too grand today,
Take heart, and climb a hill instead;
When dawn brings shroud of gloom,
I say, It's alright to stay tucked in bed.

Like a winter's bite, a shower may sting
And the thought of a bath just brings a frown.
Unwashed, unbrushed, just doing your thing
Wrapped in your fluffiest dressing gown.

It's okay to pause for a moment's peace
Indulge in take- away haven't had time to shop
Your mind won't freeze from a ceaseless lease
But your body needs rest - it's been non- stop !

The mountain will remain, steadfast and true,
When you're ready to climb once again,
Go at your pace, there's no rush to pursue,
Just love yourself until then!

What's Going Down?

Forty seven years of my life and still
I'm trying to get up that great big hill - of hope
To reach my true destination.

I realised quickly along the way
To hold to your dreams - don't let them stray
They need my spark and creation.

But I cry sometimes - ever since you've died
Doubt and worry filling up inside
Learned Life can be really tough.
But I'm truly loved by the family of mine
Knowing this makes me feel just fine,
Realising I am enough.

So I say…. Hey!
Hey! What's going down?

And I think- oh how I overthink
Every situation!
So I drink - a large alcoholic drink
To seek some relaxation!

When I was sixteen, I used to sing this song
Not a care in the world- I saw nothing wrong
But then reality hit.
My rose- tinted specs are covered in mud
Trust and gullible ran away as fast they could
With my smile and some wit.

But I cry sometimes when I'm lying in bed
Doubt and worry filling up my head
As Life can be so cruel,
But I'll smile again when I awake next day,
Knowing that you would want me to be okay .
Be happy and nobody's fool.

So I say…. Hey!
Hey! What's going down?

Forty seven years of my life and still
I'm trying to get up that great big hill of hope
To reach my true destination.

(Inspired from the song by 4 Non- Blondes)

Managing Emotions

"May the flowers remind you why the rain was necessary."

The Ballad of the Storm Maker

In a world of calm, a bold beat disrupts,
A thunderous rhythm-serenity it interrupts.
Singing accusations rise, fast and fierce,
Their threatening tones, the silence pierce.

Allegations snap, like an alligator's jaws,
Their off-beat rhythm -no breath or pause.
Lyrics loud and loose -lipped , take flight,
In a crescendo lashing like lightning's light.

An overture of opinions, offensive they seem,
Brings forth from your eyes, a tearful stream.
The pounding of injustice, hard and untrue,
Creates a pulse that is entirely new.

You ride the rapid rhythm, a rollercoaster ride,
To a song screaming the storm-maker's pride.
This turbulent tune might make you feel,
Like dancing in the rain or wailing with zeal.

Such is the song of the storm-maker's might,
Inscribed in the heart of the stormy night.
A tale that the dancer has so well told,
A tale of thunder, of accusations bold.

Medellin Menopause

Perspiring pores pour…
Manic moods make meltdowns
Like a turbulent teenage tantrum.
My marbles are misplaced not lost

Please don't stoke my fire
With your rolling eyes
And irritated impatience!

There is no rhyme or reason-
No pre-warning or triggers.
Any answers that are acceptable
Diagnosed mad and menopausal,
Emotional and exasperated,
Bloated and bewildered,
Glowing and grumpy,
Fed-up and frazzled,
Perspiring and puffed-up
But …

My Pulse is still Powerful.
My senses are stimulated
My thoughts still think! …

Men - o - pause …

Oh -Is this when we 'pause' from men?
Or is it just a time where Men should pause before they speak?

Unless they are going through the man-a-pause aka midlife crisis!

Why is ageing a crisis anyway?

Rhythm of the Rain

Some days the rain comes
Pouring out pain
Showering sensitivity
Dripping with despair
Leaking out love that's lost
Beating down, breaking hearts
Spraying sadness and sincerity
With it's pulsing 'pitter patter'
Pounding on positive thoughts
Solemnly soaking your soul
With a sombre song.

But this storm's symphony
Will stop.

The rhythm of the rain
Isn't your soul's soundtrack.

Destined for Heaven

An innocent soul, snatched too soon,
From our existence, against the moon.
In our hearts, you etched a mark,
A melody sung in the silence dark.

Once an angel on earthly ground,
In the guise of my mother, I was found.
No feathery wings, yet a radiant light,
A lioness fierce, in love and might.

A heart as vast as the fiery sphere,
Full of wisdom, comfort, and cheer.
A playful spirit, a joyous sunbeam,
In our life's canvas, you were the dream.

An ear that listened, a voice that cheered,
In stranger's crowd, you disappeared.
Yet among us, your confidence unfurled,
Putting us first, in this vast world.

Your presence, a constant comforting layer,
In our lives, you were always there.
But the divine had a different view,
A shorter earthly stint you knew.

Destined for heaven, your path was chosen,
To assist others, in struggles woven.
Our angel, our mother, our eternal love,
Now you guide us, from the skies above.

Flowers No Longer Grow Here

Such a beautiful and perfect garden
Tendered from your care and love
Now a jungle of tangles and twists,
Life's lawnmower needs a mighty shove!

The clocks stopped when you left
Stealing my confidence and sanity
Struggling to manage emotions
Questioning the purpose of humanity

Darkness creeps in at night
My thoughts that once were seeds
Become bitter , spiteful and hateful
Providing the nutrients for weeds.

Yet I 'soldier' on , digging and smiling
Telling a different story through my eyes
Feeling the hole I dig, swallowing me up
'I'm fine ' I say - but it's all just lies

My garden's no longer perfect
The holes are there to stay
Flowers no longer grow here
With rain, they grow in a different way.

The Sea's Rebellion

Oh, the sea, she doesn't like to be restrained,
In her vastness, voluminous and unchained.
With arms spread wide, she makes her claim,
Sending frothy waves, in a timeless game.

A dance with sand and shingle, rippling free,
Under the solemn gaze of the moon, eternally.
Yesterday, she was calm, charmed by the sun's soft touch,
Creating hopeful shimmers, that meant so much.

But when night falls, the solemn returns,
To control her, a fact that burns.
How dare he try to tame her might?
She, who is wild and free, ready to fight.

Rage, oh rage against the hypnotic motion,
The repetitive expectations, devoid of emotion.
Crash against the barriers and boundaries plan
For they are not meant for her, the sea's lifespan.

She is a force, uncontrolled, untamed,
A spirit that cannot be named.
Rise and fall, ebb and flow,
In the moonlight's solemn glow.

I'd Rather...

I'd rather play
Than tidy away
I'd rather dream
Than make the house gleam
I'd rather you stay
Than see you another day
I'd rather laugh
Than scrub the bath
I'd rather enjoy this treat
Than watch what I eat
I'd rather drink tea
Than make the house look twee
I'd rather buy the shoes
Than stand in supermarket queues
I'd rather wear a bright colour
Than dress in something duller
I'd rather read this book
Than the tea- start to cook
I'd rather write words that rhyme
Than waste anymore time
I'd rather plant flowers
Than work for hours
I'd rather explore
Than mop the floor
I'd rather act delirious
Than be always serious
I'd rather dance
Than give you another chance
I'd rather sing out loud

Than act all proud
I'd rather write it all down
Than constantly frown
I'd rather share good news
Than sing the blues
I'd rather walk barefoot in the sand
Than eat something bland
I'd rather have a rant and rave
Than always behave
I'd rather drink a large glass of wine
Then pretend that 'I'm fine!'
I'd rather sit and cuddle
Than unravel clothes in a muddle
I'd rather spice up my life
Instead of moaning and strife
I'd rather come off twitter
Than always feel bitter
I'd rather feel a little scared
Than always be prepared
I'd rather be a risk taker
Than a heartbreaker
I'd rather get lost in lust
Than start to dust
I'd rather listen to you snore
Than act like a bore
Life's too short
To do what I ought!

Hater's Gonna Hate!

Please tell me how it feels
To feel permanently bitter and hateful
I'm trying my best to understand
Why aren't you empathetic or grateful?

You have so much to be thankful about,
But would rather compare yourself to me
And tear strips off my situation
With no consideration or integrity!

So it's fun to rain on my parade?
Instead of joining in the celebration.
The green - eyed monster is out to play
To destroy and belittle with deliberation

Some may say my words are wasted
And 'haters gonna hate'
And if anything is going well for you,
It just makes you feel irate!

So play your game of nastiness
Negativity and criticism in all you do
But no one is impressed or upset,
And the sadness I feel- is for you!

What on Earth!?

Oh, how can we dance in harmony's bliss,
When our home is met with a reckless kiss?
Do humans not see, do they not understand,
The wounds they inflict with their destructive hand?

How can we nurture the world's serene peace,
When chaos and ruin refuse to cease?
Greedily taking, with no thought of return,
Impacting evolution- now construction does churn.

How can we bask in joy's warm embrace,
When creatures are dying from this race?
Swallowing plastic in the azure sea,
'Recycling,' you say, but it's falsehood, I see.

What on Earth do we think we're doing?
Warnings ignored, our future -we're ruining.
Extinction, destruction, the globe's warming heat,
Could we be next? The human race meets defeat?

Yet, in the heart of despair, there's a glimmer of hope,
In the hands of our youth, facing problems, to cope.
May they rise, listen, and boldly take action,
To foster an Earth with eco-friendly satisfaction.

Civilised Chaos!

Mankind emerged and developed
Intellectually civilised
Technology minded.
Moving mountains,
Building turrets and towers
Exploring, discovering,
Orbiting into space.
Hungry human computers , seeking power.

These primates, can now nurture
Empathise and philosophise.
A depressed, yet emotionally intelligent,
Overthinking and anxious society.

We compare, Judge, criticise and compete
Playing a life- long game of 'survival of the fittest'
But the rules change and are adapted for the
privileged and popular players.

But don't forget to be kind - said the person who
needs to tell everyone that they are a 'people person'.

Put everyone else's feelings first before you are
labelled selfish- but yet stereotypically allowed and
expected to be wealthy or famous when you are
self-centred.

So civilised we all are now - adapting to
A screen-lived , modern environment.

Globally communicating internationally, daily.
Yet the animal still pounces from Pandora's box, the
one that still slaughters its prey,
Thrives in the fittest of the rat race,
Runs from life's dangers,
Aggressively defends itself,
Hates and starts war,
Discriminates, segregates,
Drops bombs-both explosive and metaphorical.

Civilised chaos!

Resilience and Risk-taking

"Life isn't about waiting for the storm to pass. It's about learning to dance in the rain."

The Paradox of Change and Peace

Peculiar is the nature of life : all about change,
Yet, it's something many resist or find it strange.
Isn't it ironic, the times we fear might cause our fall - or so it seems,
Are the ones that break us open, help to follow our dreams.

We fear the storm, we fear the night,
Yet it's the darkness that helps to find our light.
In the most challenging times , we find our essence,
Blossoming into beings of resilience and presence.

So many greetings bring wishes of peace,
"Peace on earth", "peace be with you" will never cease.
But peace itself is a concept so vast,
It's more than war's absence, more than tolerance cast.

Peace is acceptance, peace is a balm,
In the face of adversity, it brings calm.
Yet, the quest for peace is ceaseless - where do we start?
For we can't find it in the world until it's in our own heart

That inner peace, that tranquil state,
It passes understanding, it opens the gate.
To a world where change is not a foe,
And peace is more than just a word we know.

May we embrace change, and in ourselves, find peace,
For only then, will our true potential ceaselessly increase.

So long Summer...

Changes whisper in the new moon,
Seasons turning to Autumn soon.
September opens her school gate,
Alarm clock set - let's not be late!

New starts for the young beginners,
No more salads, we need hot dinners.
Experienced travellers , take new paths
Ditch cold showers for bubbly baths.

Turn the page -next chapter life readers,
A new harvest to plough for hungry feeders
Blue sky's to soar for a migrating bird.
Crunching and rustling of leaves to be heard

Carefree days are accurately timed,
Free verse is now organised and rhymed,
Memories of lapping up golden rays ,
Are wrapped and knitted in cooler days,

Holiday blues, wipe away that tear,
This golden time shines - have no fear,
Amber beauty and in this fallen song,
Summertime waves goodbye- So long

Flying High

Just like fleeting moments, now past,
Once, you were a babe in my arms, so vast.

My heart's most cherished treasure,
Lost in your blue eyes - a measureless pleasure.

Knowing you are mine, my dear,
As your mother, my wishes are clear.

May happiness be your constant mate,
And may you chase your dreams, however late.

Proud I am, of your relentless strive,
And the doors of opportunities, you've contrived.

The thought of you leaving the nest,
Tugs at my emotional strings with zest.

New ventures may soon be on your chart,
Flying from home, but never from my heart.

The Rise of the Woman Warrior

There will be times a head my dear,
When you are succumbed to fear,
Grief, failure, rejection : hitting a brick wall,
So head up, shoulders back and stand tall.

Anxiety and stress may cloud your sight,
Self- doubt is your friend in the still of the night.
No ray of light seems to be visible,
Feed your loneliness to this beast so terrible.

In the deepest, darkest abyss,
sadness tries to give you her kiss
Never lose hold of the hope in your heart,
It's the lamp in the dark, your morning start.

Don't be disheartened, don't stoop so low,
Sinking in the depths of despair and sorrow.
Have faith - time passes quickly my friend,
Soon all of your pains will come to an end.

So strong and brave - the warrior is you,
Inner strength, rising above the pain so true.
This wounded soldier- victorious in the end,
Standing tall amidst the aura of a legend.

So, rise again, oh woman warrior
Those who cross you couldn't be sorrier.
Spiritually brave and bright, standing tall
Ferocious female warrior, admired by all.

Thrills and Chills

Scares are apparently good for you
Every once in a while,
Heart rate heightened , pulse pumping
Screams , succeeded by a smile.

Riding roller coasters reap a rush,
Climbing, dropping, looping
Adrenaline levels increase so high
Soaring, flying, swooping!

Dark nights creep in like a sinister cat,
Casting shadows in the moonlight
Spooky settings write haunted stories
Imagination reacts with fright

Artificial fear from a scare fest
Thankfully no monsters or kills!
Screams spontaneously stop silence
Created by the chills and thrills.

Gradually Healing

Healing is a traumatic journey
One that may take much time.
For it's a tender and raw process,
That cannot be rushed to prime.

Some days there are blue skies
Ushering a soothing chime,
But suddenly a storm thunders
And you're the lightning's crime.

But stay strong and fear not,
For the sun will shine once more,
The rain and wind's dance will end
After the storm has given its final roar.

No longer the same, but still beautiful
Healing all the parts that were once torn,
A unique, stunning and stronger design
Birthing a new you, reborn.

Through the healing, you'll find strength
Restoring hope, replacing fear,
Taking in more light, more love than before,
A rainbow remains, after the tear.

Happiness and Harmony

"Let your smile change the world, but don't let the world change your smile."

Harmoniously Hopeful

Hope is what I cling to
At times when life is tough.
Resiliently persevering , though
My body has had enough.
Only hope can prevent forced fatality
Not yet will the finale music play.
You bring harmony to my life's song.

Bucket List Epiphany

It's true what they say,
Time really does fly.
Before you know it
Opportunities pass by.

In my youth, I dreamed
With boundless zest,
Creating a bucket list,
Now a humble quest.

Places I desired to see
Goals I wanted to achieve
Adamant that it would happen
I had to hope and believe

Much of it came true
By hard work and pure grit
But challenges and changes
Have altered and adapted it.

Many years have passed
Since I have thought of this list.
But there are no regrets or a time
I think of what I've missed.

Adventures within your lifetime
To be great-don't have to be grand
You may desire exotic and spicy
But essentials may need to be bland.

Your life time goals and aspirations
Don't need to reach the highest peak
Merely moments that touch the soul.
Make your life special and unique.

The love bestowed from my husband
Sunny walks by the ocean's side,
Family times full of love and laughter
Watching my daughters grow with pride.

There is no deadline to achieve dreams
And if I visit places - let it be with you
Being loved as a wife and a mother
Fills my bucket - Is my only list -it's true.

Autumn Daze

Confused by the contrasts, Autumn brings-
An amber glow creates a dream-like daze.
Grey skies bring soaking shivers,
That interrupt golden bursts,
Between stark branches
Where feet crunch-
Crispy, cascading, crimson tree feathers.
Knitted garments create cosiness,
Warming wetness , shielding strong breezes.
Chilli adds spice to pumpkin soup,
Adding flavour to dreariness
As darkness creeps back in ,
To gate-crash the afternoon
Bringing the Sunset
Along to rise earlier
That lights for migrating birds

Derbyshire Hiking Hysteria

Adventures with my mate Ange
They are always so much fun!
We always have such a laugh
Come wind, rain or in the glorious sun.

So off we went to Derbyshire,
Starting in the picturesque Hathersage,
Following a route on Ange's walking APP
Fields and rocky hills, set a stunning stage

Admiring the amazing scenery,
The walk started off so well
Until we start climbing …
Over a slippy stile I fell!

Not landing on grass - but rock
In this ever inclining , fern covered path
After pulling me up- checking I was ok..
That's when Ange began to laugh!

After a few choice words, I was giggling too,
Bruised , broken nail and a stinging pain,
As between the rocks were nettles,
Well they do say- no pain- no gain!!!

We came so well prepared…not
Not a snack or enough water to drink
The APP now tells us it's a 5 hour walk
This wounded soldier was on the brink!

Making it to the top of cliff- photo stop
The wind blows us along,
Thinking it will be easier to get back,
But oh no - I was so wrong!

Another hysterical moment,
Was watching me climb down
Yes I'm sliding on my bottom,
Is the pub there - I can see the town!

Dehydrated and almost running
'Quicker' she says - I'm resisting a strop
But then she passes me her water,
Letting me have her last drop.

Fourteen kilometres later (I'm not fit!)
A well earned beer and bath,
Giggling at the photos of a great day
Shattering -but a right good laugh!

November Nights

Watch as the seasons change
Casting shadows-sinister and strange
Flames flicker from faces of coal,
Remembering seasons of the soul.

Nights as black as a writer's ink.
Poppy shrouded cenotaph - stop to think
Heavy rain floods a saddened heart
Frosty mornings need a caffeine start.

Firework skies bring sparkle and magic
A gunpowder plot with an aim to be tragic.
Moonlight casts a melancholy mood
Boosted by baking and homemade food

Rocking Out!

Guitars roared like an angry lion,
Through the bright blazing lights,
Igniting thousands of flames,
Burning and leaping in dancing fights.

The music fills my whole being,
It's sound washes over me,
Singing with a passion inside
Releasing restless energy.

A singer howls into the night sky,
Gently swaying crowds begin jumping,
As a song is greeted by a sea of arms,
Clapping along to a drumbeat thumping.

Exhilaration- feeling wild and free!
My veins pump with rock and roll.
The rush of adrenaline and excitement
Essential food to feed a rockers soul.

Hibernating Heart

December drums her merry tune,

A melody of merriment and festivities.
Lit-up , glowing and glittering,
Cold nights leave us jittering,
Hearts warmed with songs and nativities.

Christmas holidays- time for a rest?
Social situations sore to new heights
Preparations are never ending
Bustling shops - so much spending!
Family gatherings, parties, late nights.

Cherished moments with loved ones
Melancholy moods , memories of the past
Such a month of mixed emotions
Muddled minds from a year's notions
Exhausted bodies fight a flu that seems to last.

Time to rest your mind, body and soul
Your hibernating heart needs to stay strong
Before the new year creeps in
And the fresh challenges begin
With a recharged pulse for a new year's song.

Gigglebox

I've laughed so much , I wipe a tear,
My smile adorning from ear to ear.
Sniggeringin your presence - I can't conceal
Chuckling is constant - this comedy's real!

Naturally humourous- it's subtle and so sunny,
Just effortless! Without trying to be funny.
No tickling required: no jesters, no trick,
Just your radiant spirit, 'taking the mick!'

Even when the skies paint a sombre hue,
You find the silver lining, the joy that's due.
When everything around is clouded in blue,
You light up my world just by being you.

Through laughter and joy, a nickname I've got,
I'm the '*Gigglebox*' -as I laugh a lot!
The reason is as simple as the morning dew,
I am a '*Gigglebox*', because of you!

Italian Adventures!

Suitcases are packed to the brim
Let our Italian adventures begin!
As we jet off to adventures new,
Many places to see - so much to do
This beautiful European destination,
Has always been a place of fascination
Time to bathe in the golden rays of the sun
Quality time with family - lots of fun!
Excited to visit a place with much history
Answer questions that have been a mystery.
Make new memories of love and laughter,
Enjoy delicious cuisine- the pizza and pasta.
Life gets busy - time to stop and be still
Switch off, breathe, relax and chill.
So ciao for now - I'm off- I'm gone!
Holiday mode is officially on!

Hope and Gratitude

"Look back in forgiveness, forward in hope, down in compassion and up in gratitude."

Grateful Gardens

So you want to change your meadow?
The grass is greener on the other side?

Or so it appears…

Sick of being stung by my nettles?
Disgruntled with me dishing the dirt?
Away ..
Go to that amazing artificial grass!
That's so green it gleams and glows.
Practically perfect
Pouting and posing
Not a blade out of place
Unlike this twisted tangle
Overgrown and out-dated.

But weeds wind their way in
You can't prevent them.
Concealed weeds will find crevices.

Don't expect to experience true emotions
Fake, bold and bristly,
Cold to touch
But wins a popularity contest
It will never give you flowers
Come rain or shine.

Perhaps this old grass
May be worn and muddy in places
But like a horse's mane, it's soft to touch
Smelling of the sweet morning dew.
Tasty to others who graze that way
Appreciated and devoured.

No more will you walk all over me
Poke holes in me
Leave me untended
Unwatered
Dried up
Unloved and cared for.

I am the lawn of a grateful gardener now.

Darling Daughters

Two gorgeous girls

A pair of precious pearls
Beautiful inside and out
Reminding me what Life's about
Each and every day.

You fill my heart with love and pride
How I've laughed and how I've cried
Tears of joy at every memory so new
You bring a smile when I'm feeling blue
In all you do and say.

To be your mum, I'm truly blessed
Since your births I've been obsessed
Through every amazing age
Enjoyed every surprise and stage
Cherished- come what may!

As a mother, I constantly worry and care
Unconditionally, I will always be there.
A love that will last a lifetime's duration
The greatest achievement, my best creation
Happy National Daughter's Day!

Sisterly Love

We may be sisters by birth - by blood
But my sister's a friend from the heart.
Love and memories make strong sisterhood
There are so many - where do I start?!

A 'Piro the clown' bedroom we shared
And a love for barbie dolls too
For our pet rabbit (Ricky)- we cared
Looking out for each other as we grew.

Our childhood was happy -full of joy
love and laughter -with very few niggles
Sure-as teenagers we set out to annoy
But it usually ended with us in giggles.

So proud to have you in my life
To see what you've accomplished
You are a lovely mum and a wife
A beautiful person who's cherished

Through hard times too - you've been there
To talk to , cry with and lend an ear,
Always honest and helpful because you care
A true friend with no judgement to fear.

Wonderfully, our families have grown to be
Just as close as we were as kids too
Devastated -mum's not here to see
But so thankful that I've always got you.

Another celebration, family fun and cake
For the world- we wouldn't miss!
Beautiful birthday memories to make
Thanks for being a wonderful sis!

Thank You For The Music

Unfortunately, I'm no longer **the girl with golden hair**

But I'm a **'Mama Mia'** with a name that's still quite rare.
Gimmie, gimmie, gimmie music- I'm a **dancing queen**
An Abba-themed west-end musical - the best I've seen!

At London's grand Novello Theatre, we joined the queue
'Don't want to be late mum!' - **knowing me, knowing you!**
Calling an **SOS**-if this rain doesn't stop - I'm cold I'm blue
Can we please have shelter - and warmth **voulez vous**?

I've been waiting for you with excited anticipation
A show based on ABBA songs- loved by the nation.
It's a wonderful treat as it costs **money, money, money**!
A present for my daughters sweeter than **honey, honey**

As the curtains rise and music fills the hall
I'm full of gratitude - as t**he winner takes it all**
Such amazing talent sent me into a stupor!
Sparkling lights, dancing like a **super trouper!**

Just like **our last summer**, so happy that I beam
So stunned and amazed- as if **I have a dream!**
But **one of us is crying** during this next song
Hey there **Chiquitita** - tell me what's wrong?

Smiling at my girls through my tears, as they know
They're **slipping through my fingers** as they grow
A song that reduces me to a blubbering state
An emotional experience - the show was so great!

But it's time to go - we've a train to catch you see
Don't worry we'll make it - **take a chance on me**
Quick grab a cab before there's a queue
Where to - you've guessed it - **Waterloo**!

To my unpoetic hubby...

Thank you for your brutal honesty
Unknowingly your feedback was right,
Your 'no frills ' - ' a spade is a spade' attitude
Makes me try harder to get it right!

You 'don't do poetry'
Yet you'll listen to me witter on
Bring me down to earth
If it's too abstract or too long

So poetry may not be your bag
It makes you roll your eyes and huff
You don't understand why I like it.
Occasionally listening to mine is enough!

But you don't fool me either
Pretending to be grumpy and a little pedantic
You might not dazzle me with words
Surprisingly - you're quite the romantic.

Opposites do attract they say
Like 'Yin and yang'- a concept that's Chinese
You keep me grounded, rock my world
And make great cups of teas!

Celebrate the Things so Great!

Life can get you down at times,
It's' not always a bed of roses,
Besides, thorns can scratch and scar,
Scents can irritate allergic noses.

But somewhere in the chaos,
When frazzled and feeling stressed,
There's still something to bring a smile,
To be thankful for and feel blessed.

So when those moments happen,
Embrace them and celebrate!
Before the next train leaves your station,
Pause, smile and enjoy this time that's great!

Some may mistake this as gloating,
As not everyone reacts in ways the same,
But happy souls will feel warm-hearted
Positivity will fuel their flickering flame.

Rock out in the thunderstorms that loudly roar,
Don't let them rain on your parade.
Bathe in the beams of light bursting through ,
Slide down the shimmering rainbow it's made.

I'll sing a song for every tough situation,
Pull out the positives from the critics
Learn the important parts from a lesson
Seek out the truth from external politics.

Work to live - not vice- versa ,
Take note of the silence- not just the loud
Stay true to myself , listen to my heart
Shout from the rooftops when I'm proud.

Dad

Oh Dad, with warmth and love you shine,
Bringing smiles and joy- divine.
Through life's ups and downs, you stand tall,
Guiding us, never letting us fall.

From the laughter in your eyes so bright,
To the wisdom in your words so right.
You're the rock that we lean on,
In times of joy and times of storm.

Your love for us, unwavering and true,
A beacon in the dark, this we always knew.
With every joke and every song,
You fill our hearts, where love belongs.

Adored by all the grandkids
Providing a 'Grandad's taxi' ride.
In their lives and in their hearts,
Full of admiration, love and pride.

So here's to you, our dear Dad,
In our hearts, you'll always be clad.
For all the memories, big and small,
Thank you for being the best of all.

Hope Springs Eternal

Never ever surrender your dreams
The past is gone - it's a memories song
But where there's life -hope springs eternal
And this helps us all to stay strong.

Good things come to a patient soul
Hope's eternal, in our hearts steady.
Anticipate the dawn of better tomorrows,
Be optimistic and kind. Be ready!

Even in poverty's shadowed hollows.
Better to be in life's bustling thread,
Dance in the wild winds and roll of thunder
Then in the silent kingdom of the dead.

Hold on, for luck may soon steer your fate,
The joy of victory may be just a week away,
Who can predict what future may unfurl
Your triumph, in splendid glory, may display.

Destiny may have greatness in store
Never let go of your life's dream,
Maintain positivity , hope and believe
Follow its path, let your spirit gleam

Maintain positivity, hope for the best,
The champion may stumble, be knocked down,
No matter what you are faced with
But they will rise, claiming victory's crown.

ABOUT THE AUTHOR

Zowie Norris is delighted to share her second poetry anthology and third published book. She also has two poems published in an international anthology and in international magazines and continues to post a weekly poem on her social media author pages.

'Barb the Bird of Hope', her first Children's book, was published in June 2021. It was at this time that she started sharing weekly poems, rekindling her passion for writing poetry and publishing her first anthology 'Poetically Positive' in June 2023.

Zowie studied English and Primary teaching at Bretton Hall College, West Yorkshire, England, graduating in 1998. Since then, she has shared her passion for creative writing with the pupils in six different primary schools in South Yorkshire, as a teacher and educational leader for the last twenty-six years.

Family is important to Zowie, who lives with her husband James and two daughters, Phoebe and Jasmine. The loss of her beloved mother, and managing anxieties around the pandemic, highlighted the importance of family, gratitude, helping others, having hope and a positive mindset.

You can follow Zowie and her poetry writing on her social media page.

https://www.facebook.com/zowienorrisauthor

https://www.instagram.com/zowie_norris_author

https://www.Twitter.com@ZowieNorris

@barbthebirdofhope22

@zowie_norris_author

If you have enjoyed my poetry, please pop me a review on Amazon and/or Goodreads. Your support is always appreciated.

Poetically Positive

A Poetry Anthology to bring hope, happiness and encourage a positive mindset

ZOWIE NORRIS

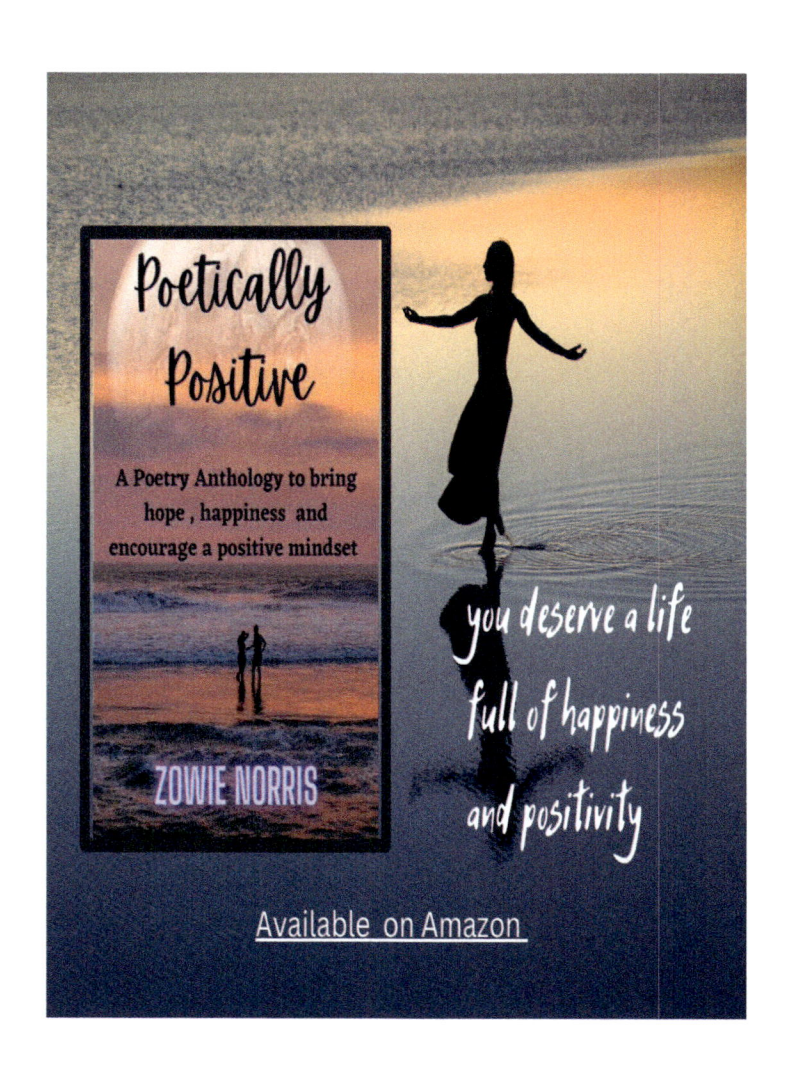

you deserve a life full of happiness and positivity

Available on Amazon

Printed in Great Britain
by Amazon